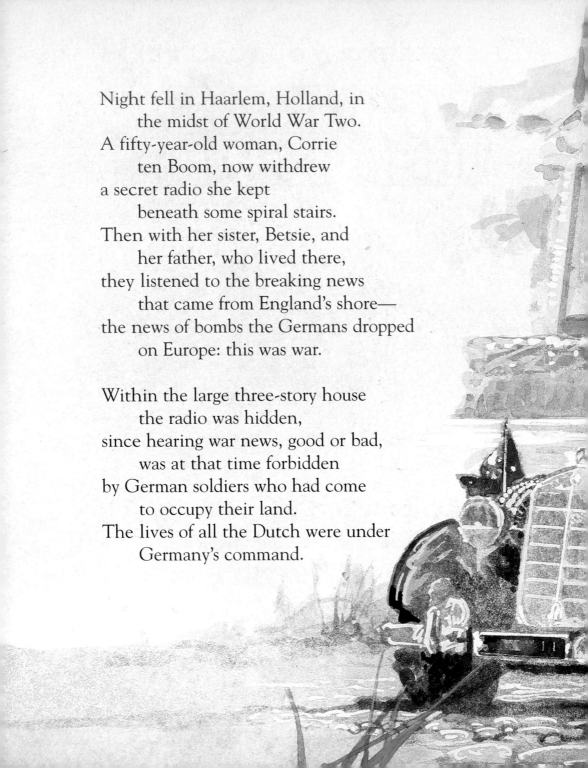

Night fell in Haarlem, Holland, in
        the midst of World War Two.
A fifty-year-old woman, Corrie
        ten Boom, now withdrew
a secret radio she kept
        beneath some spiral stairs.
Then with her sister, Betsie, and
        her father, who lived there,
they listened to the breaking news
        that came from England's shore—
the news of bombs the Germans dropped
        on Europe: this was war.

Within the large three-story house
        the radio was hidden,
since hearing war news, good or bad,
        was at that time forbidden
by German soldiers who had come
        to occupy their land.
The lives of all the Dutch were under
        Germany's command.

Upon the first floor of the house
    the Ten Booms had a shop.
They worked on watches and repaired
    some old and broken clocks.

All day and night they heard the steady
    ticking of the time.
As days passed by, they longed for peace
    on earth among mankind.

One night they heard a person knocking
    hard on their front door.
They opened it. A Jewish neighbor
    held a bag and wore
what looked like five full sets of clothes.
    Her eyes looked terrified.
She stood there shaking, silent; Corrie
    ushered her inside.

Most Jews had been imprisoned and
    so many of them died,
and those still free were searching for
    a place where they could hide.

Now Corrie knew the German Nazis
    deeply disliked Jews.
She also knew the course of action
    she would have to choose,
for Corrie was a Christian; she
    could not just turn away.
She and her family bravely chose
    to let this woman stay.

Another woman came, with children;
    they, too, were her guests.
Yet Corrie knew, by hiding them,
    she likely risked arrest.

One day a Jewish woman brought
    her baby, small and weak.
The baby cried. The frightened mother
    found it hard to speak.

So when a minister arrived
    to get his watch repaired,
it seemed to Corrie he was sent
    in answer to her prayers.

His house was more secluded; they'd
    be safer there with him.
She asked if he would take the baby
    and the mother in.

"No, no!" he said instinctively.
    His fear showed in his eyes.
"That Jewish baby could cost all
    of us our very lives."

Although he was a Christian man
    and knew the Jews' grim plight,
some Christians were too scared to do
    what Corrie knew was right.

Though disappointed, Corrie found
    the next best place to stay,
much farther from her busy street,
    more safe, out of harm's way.

Soon Corrie thought that she should add
 a place for Jews to hide
within her home in case the Germans
 searched the house inside.

A famous architect arrived.
 He set to work and soon
he'd built upstairs, near Corrie's bed,
 a hidden, secret room.

One quiet night in winter after
 Corrie fell asleep,
she woke up to an urgent cry
 and sounds of rushing feet.

She looked up at her Jewish friends.
 Their eyes revealed their dread.
"The Germans are downstairs," one gasped,
 as Corrie leapt from bed.

She opened up her closet, pulled
    a handle down, and then
the wall slid back; the secret door
    led to her "Angels' Den."

"Oh hurry! Hurry!" Corrie urged.
    The Jews stepped in the space.
Then Corrie slid the wall back to
    conceal the small, safe place.

She shut the closet door, jumped back
    in bed, and shut her eyes.
In seconds when a German came
    she tried to act surprised.

He ordered her downstairs, and in
      the clock shop, grabbed her arm,
and made her stand against the wall.
      As Corrie looked alarmed,
he asked, "Where did you hide the Jews?"
      When Corrie would not speak,
he slapped her right across the face.
      She felt her legs grow weak.

No matter what he did to her,
      no matter how he yelled,
she would not give the Jews away;
      though scared, she would not tell.

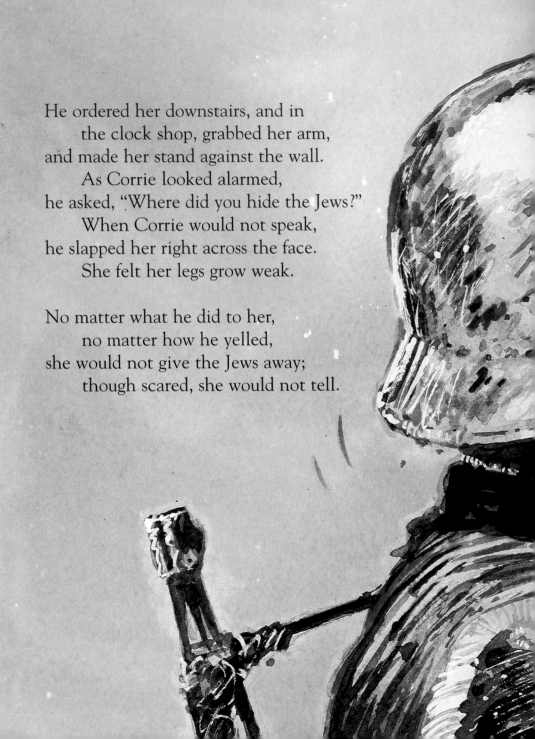

Although the soldiers smashed through walls
　　　the Jews could not be found.
The Ten Booms were arrested and
　　　in handcuffs they were bound
and taken to a prison that
　　　was cold and dark inside.
Just ten days later Papa ten Boom
　　　grew so ill he died.

When Corrie read the Bible in
　　　her cell, it eased her fear.
It made her feel a sense of peace
　　　to know that God was near.

And then she got a letter saying
　　　all the "clocks" were safe.
This code word meant the Jews had safely
　　　left the hiding place.

That summer, guards shoved Corrie and
    her sister on a train;
the boxcars sped to Germany
    to camps where they'd remain.

Packed in with eighty women, they
    all struggled to get air.
There were no seats or windows, only
    darkness and despair.

Their journey finally ended after
    three long fearful nights.
The famished women gasped for air
    and squinted in the light.

They soon were forced to climb a slope
　　though all were weak and ill.
As Corrie saw what was below
　　it made her stop, stock-still.

She saw long rows of clapboard buildings
　　painted ugly gray.
A wall with sharp barbed wire would
　　enclose them night and day.

"It's Ravensbruck, a women's prison,"
　　one voice softly said.
"I've heard it's bad there," said another
　　as she stared ahead.

But Betsie said to Corrie as
　　they stumbled down the hill,
"No pit's so deep that God's great love
　　will not be deeper still."

The words reminded Corrie of
　　her Bible, and she thought,
I have to hide it somewhere or
　　I'll lose it if I'm caught.

So when the women lined up for
    a head to toe inspection,
she prayed, *God, send your angels here.*
    Please give me your protection.

As Corrie watched, a soldier searched
    the woman just ahead,
and then he reached past Corrie, searching
    those behind instead!

With Betsie and a thousand other
    women she was sent
to live inside a barracks that
    was filled with filth and stench.

Because of all the fleas inside
    the guards would not come near,
and so the Ten Booms read God's Word
    aloud there with no fear.

Months later Betsie grew so sick
        some wondered if she'd live.
But her abiding faith in God
        kept Betsie positive.

She spoke of being free by New
        Year's—only weeks away,
and Corrie then would hold her and
        together they would pray.

She also said that when the war
        had ended they'd discover
that displaced persons all around
        would need help to recover.

They'd need a temporary place,
    which Betsie would describe:
a home with landscaped gardens and
    with large old trees outside.

The home she saw had marble statues
    set into its walls.
The rooms were clean and spacious and
    the windows wide and tall.

At roll call, Betsie fainted in
    the yard one snowy day,
collapsing on the frozen ground;
    soon guards dragged her away.

They took her to the hospital.
    Soon Corrie sneaked inside
and there heard Betsie's favorite words
    before her sister died:
"No pit's so deep," she said again,
    her voice now small but sure,
"that God's great love's not deeper still—
    His great love will endure."

Days later, Corrie was surprised
when—unlike many Jews—
she learned that she would be released—
miraculous good news.

And on December twenty-eighth
before the New Year's Day,
as Betsie said, they both were free,
each one in her own way.

On May eighth, nineteen forty-five,
    the radio brought news:
all Holland was now free again,
    as Germany withdrew.

As Betsie had predicted, there
    were people everywhere
who'd lost their families, homes, and jobs
    and needed help and care.

And soon the home of Betsie's dreams
    was helping those in need.
The house was given like God's grace:
    without a charge, for free.

The years passed by, and Corrie died
    when she was ninety-one.
Her life blessed many people through
    the brave, kind deeds she'd done.

Though she had known the suffering of
    the deepest, darkest pit,
she'd also known the deeper love
    of God through all of it,
and that was why she risked her life
    to do just what was right:
so God's great love could flow through her
    and shine out in the night.

Christian Heroes: Then & Now

by Janet and Geoff Benge

Adoniram Judson: Bound for Burma
Amy Carmichael: Rescuer of Precious Gems
Betty Greene: Wings to Serve
Brother Andrew: God's Secret Agent
Cameron Townsend: Good News in Every Language
Clarence Jones: Mr. Radio
Corrie ten Boom: Keeper of the Angels' Den
Count Zinzendorf: Firstfruit
C. S. Lewis: Man, Myth, and Imagination
C. T. Studd: No Retreat
David Livingstone: Africa's Trailblazer
Eric Liddell: Something Greater Than Gold
Florence Young: Mission Accomplished
George Müller: The Guardian of Bristol's Orphans
Gladys Aylward: The Adventure of a Lifetime
Hudson Taylor: Deep in the Heart of China
Ida Scudder: Healing Bodies, Touching Hearts
Jim Elliot: One Great Purpose
John Wesley: The World as His Parish
John Williams: Messenger of Peace
Jonathan Goforth: An Open Door in China
Lillian Trasher: The Greatest Wonder in Egypt
Loren Cunningham: Into All the World
Lottie Moon: Giving Her All for China
Mary Slessor: Forward into Calabar
Nate Saint: On a Wing and a Prayer
Rachel Saint: A Star in the Jungle
Rowland Bingham: Into Africa's Interior
Sundar Singh: Footprints Over the Mountains
Wilfred Grenfell: Fisher of Men
William Booth: Soup, Soap, and Salvation
William Carey: Obliged to Go

Heroes for Young Readers and *Heroes of History for Young Readers* are based on the *Christian Heroes: Then & Now* and *Heroes of History* biographies by Janet and Geoff Benge. Don't miss out on these exciting, true adventures for ages ten and up!

Continued on the next page...

Heroes of History
by Janet and Geoff Benge

Abraham Lincoln: A New Birth of Freedom
Benjamin Franklin: Live Wire
Christopher Columbus: Across the Ocean Sea
Clara Barton: Courage under Fire
Daniel Boone: Frontiersman
Douglas MacArthur: What Greater Honor
George Washington Carver: From Slave to Scientist
George Washington: True Patriot
Harriet Tubman: Freedombound
John Adams: Independence Forever
John Smith: A Foothold in the New World
Laura Ingalls Wilder: A Storybook Life
Meriwether Lewis: Off the Edge of the Map
Orville Wright: The Flyer
Theodore Roosevelt: An American Original
Thomas Edison: The Inventor
William Penn: Liberty and Justice for All

...and more coming soon. Unit study curriculum guides are also available.

Heroes for Young Readers Activity Guides
Educational and Character-Building Lessons for Children
by Renee Taft Meloche

Heroes for Young Readers Activity Guide for Books 1–4
Gladys Aylward, Eric Liddell, Nate Saint, George Müller

Heroes for Young Readers Activity Guide for Books 5–8
Amy Carmichael, Corrie ten Boom, Mary Slessor, William Carey

Heroes for Young Readers Activity Guide for Books 9–12
Betty Greene, David Livingstone, Adoniram Judson, Hudson Taylor

Heroes for Young Readers Activity Guide for Books 13–16
Jim Elliot, Cameron Townsend, Jonathan Goforth, Lottie Moon

...and more coming soon.

Designed to accompany the vibrant Heroes for Young Readers books, these fun-filled activity guides lead young children through a variety of character-building and educational activities. Pick and choose from the activities or follow the included thirteen-week syllabus. An audio CD with book readings, songs, and fun activity tracks is available for each Activity Guide.

For a free catalog of books and materials contact
YWAM Publishing, P.O. Box 55787, Seattle, WA 98155
1-800-922-2143, www.ywampublishing.com